James Stevenson

DODD, MEAD & COMPANY
New York

1   2   3   4   5   6   7   8   9   10

Of the 122 drawings in this book, 115 appeared originally in *The
New Yorker* and were copyrighted © in 1958, 1959, 1960, 1961,
1964, and in the years 1966 through 1978, inclusive,
by the New Yorker Magazine, Inc.

Library of Congress Cataloging in Publication Data

Stevenson, James, date
Let's boogie!

1. American wit and humor, Pictorial. I. Title.
NC1429.S65A4   1978   741.5'973   78-17558
ISBN 0-396-07633-5

To Frank Modell
(*at his insistence*)

"*It's me again.*"

"*Would you like to freshen up?*"

"*Inca dinka do . . .*"

"*Call the photographers. I'm going out to romp with my dog.*"

AND DISPERSE

"Morning, sweetheart."

"Would you like to see my pile?"

"Wouldn't it be enough just not to return their invitation?"

"*No ideas for you at the moment, but I have mentioned your name to somebody at the National Endowment for the Arts.*"

HEY, MISTER HOW BOUT A LIL HELP — I USTA BE IN PITCHAS...

"Night, dear."

"*Let me see if I have it correctly, sir. To hell with the appetizer. A chopped sirloin that damn well better be rare. No goddam relish tray. Who cares which salad dressing, since they all taste like sludge?*"

"*This is the worst Brahms First I've _ever_ heard.*"

"Our colleague Professor Bodley has been appearing on several what I
believe are called 'talk shows' in connection with his new book."

"Why don't we just have leftovers tonight?"

"Well, here it is, honey. The bottom line."

" 'Patchy fog this morning, clearing by midday.' "

1

3

2

4

"I don't like it already."

"*Frankly, I never dreamed the World Trade Center would get finished so quickly and without incident.*"

FREEZE-FRAMES, 1944

Planes flew right over the roof.

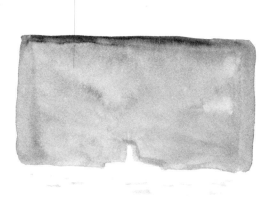

Submarines came up near the beach.

A sailor lay bleeding in the street near the bar.

Grandma listened to Raymond Gram swing.

The U.S.O. sent two soldiers for dinner.

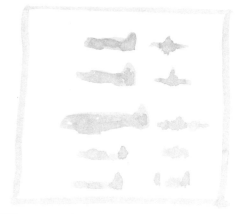

We memorized the shapes of German and Japanese aircraft.

There was a lot of kale in our victory garden.

We learned to jitterbug to Tommy Dorsey's "Boogie Woogie."

Sally didn't want to go all the way. (Nobody did.)

Don's cousin had his picture in *Life*.

Mr. Travis knew somebody who sold him meat.

We talked about whether we'd be able to stand up under interrogation if we got captured.

It was fun opening Spam.

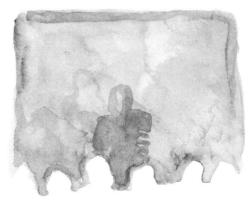

An admiral gave a talk on how it was going over there.

From the high meadow people watched for enemy planes.

A stranger might be a saboteur.

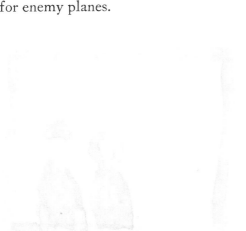

We didn't know what to say to Mr. and Mrs. Warren; their son was killed in Italy.

Everything would be better once the war was over.

"*And help me find a job with a more creative agency.*"

"*Now, on this one, Your Majesty, you'll note the heavy velours for autumn comfort with the luxurious silk pile lining and the matching royal monogram and piping.*"

"Confound it, Moxley! Any more of that and I'll have you drummed out of the Sierra Club!"

"Hey, do we have strawberries crushed in cream cheese?"

"*I'm sick of the whole approach. Just tell the public we're cold and aloof and we make a goddam good carburetor.*"

"Well, as of today I'm a free agent and can sign with anybody I want."

"*You know what bugs me? Everybody I know is wizened.*"

"We noticed a glut of tennis camps, music camps, wilderness camps—
and suddenly a real need became obvious."

"He was a *nice* Pharaoh."

"You're a disgrace to the Highway Department, Hagerty!"

"*Don't give me that!*"

"The social fabric is extremely fragile around here."

"So *that's* where it goes! Well, I'd like to thank you fellows for bringing this
to my attention."

"*Let's hear it for the bouillabaisse!*"

"*Leonard isn't going anywhere. It's just the way he always observes Labor Day.*"

"Oh, it's you! I thought I heard ruffles and flourishes."

"*But, dear, I thought you <u>wanted</u> it shaped like a pyramid.*"

" 'Sunset,' by Herbert W. Brockway . . ."

"For a little extra we could have got Giotto."

"Let's face it, Larry. You're not a key player."

"*I fear, sire, we have the wrong Michelangelo.*"

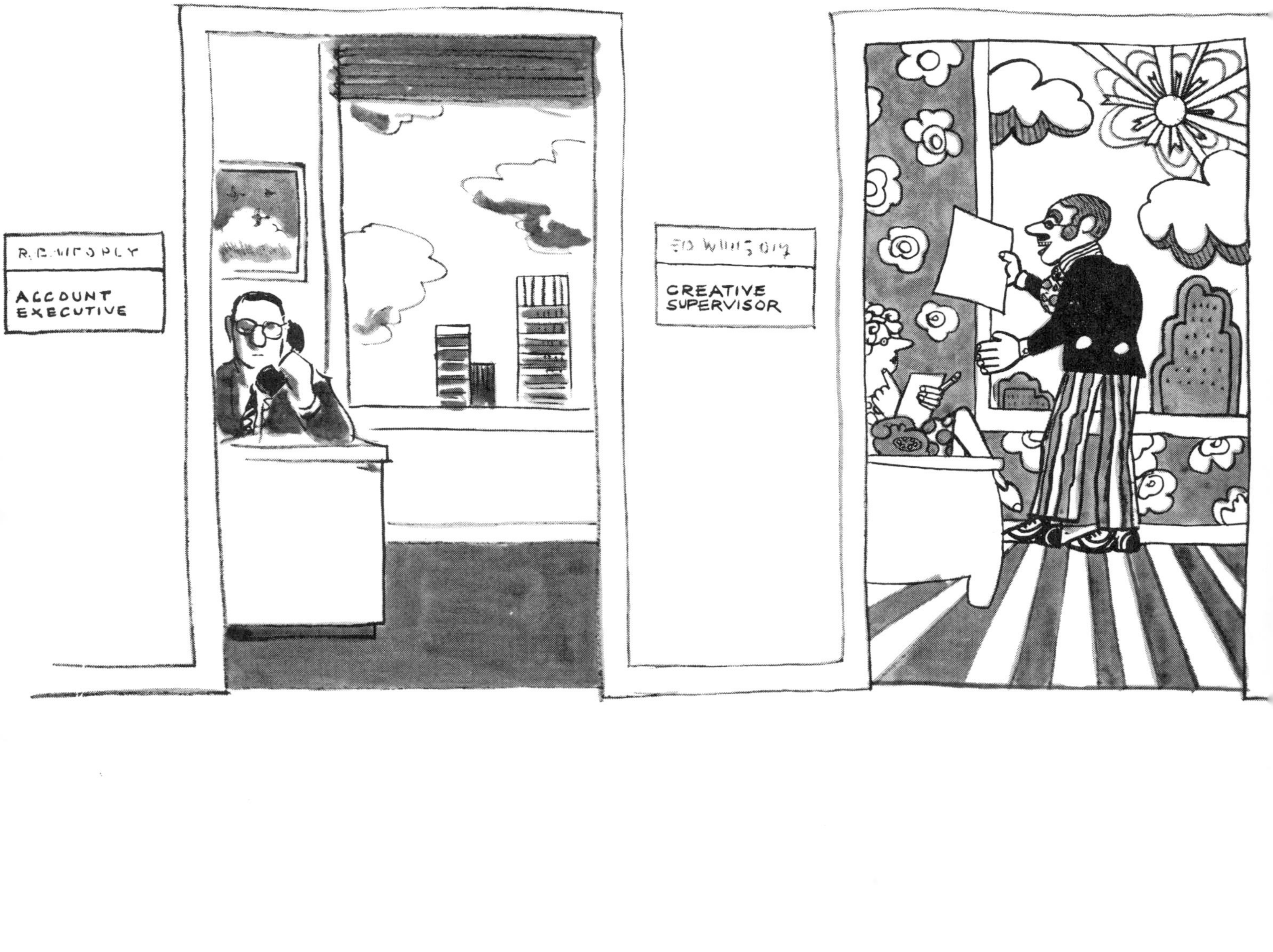
ACCOUNT EXECUTIVE
CREATIVE SUPERVISOR

"She's done a remarkable job over the years, considering."

BARTLETT'S FAMILIAR QUOTATIONS

In May, 1855, in Cambridge, Massachusetts, John Bartlett, proprietor of the university bookstore, completed the first edition of his book, and began to write the preface:

"The object of this work is to show, to some extent, the obligations our language owes to various authors for numerous phrases . . ."

"... and ..."

6

8

". . . familiar quotations which have become 'household words.'"

"Oh, I don't know. I guess maybe increased service to others, more generosity and less selfishness, full participation in public affairs on the state and local levels, greater dedication to my work and my family. What are your New Year's resolutions?"

"No, I think it goes like this. Two men carrying three packs come to a stream. There is a canoe, but it will only carry *one* man and *one* pack . . ."

"Top drawer, that chap. Who else would think of waving goodbye?"

"And now it's time once more for Julia Child."

"*I knew it! Sir Eric hasn't the guts to come out when there's real fighting!*"

"*It's known as the Isle of Cancelled Sitcoms.*"

"As of September 1st, I'm sorry to say, you will all be replaced by a tiny chip of silicon."

"It seems only yesterday they were giving away crystal stemware."

"Make like you're Socrates."

"*Brooks Brothers? Arthur T. Sturgis here. I believe a mistake has been made.*"

"*I just never imagined they wouldn't finally come up with <u>some</u> form of government aid.*"

"What else did you bring me?"

"Well, this initial test suggests that the authenticity of your Rembrandt may be questionable."

"*I'm sorry. The shell you have picked up is not a working seashell. I'm sorry. The shell . . .*"

"*I am no revisionist, but yet I never fail to wonder. Where in the world did we get these weird chairs?*"

STEVENSON

"*Our revels now are ended. I've got to get up early tomorrow.*"

"*I can't decide whether to fish or cut bait.*"

"You call this cuisine _haute_, Mac?"

"I think it fair to say, Mr. Webster, that we are the most Chekhovian household in East Hampton."

"Sorry, kids. You're punk, but you're just not punk enough."

"*I must say this was the worst-led migration I've ever been on in my life.*"

"*I was grinding out barnyards and farmhouses and cows in the meadow, and then, suddenly, I figured to hell with it.*"

"*Heaven knows, Alice, I've tried to make you happy.*"

"...and blues are plentiful in Block Island Sound. Now, with a special report
on stripers, here's my colleague, Lem Witherspoon."

"Let's take it again from 'klonk.'"

"It's the most blatant violation of park rules I've ever seen."

"Sung dynasty—960-1280."

"*Go to hell!*"

"*That banquet was most delicious, and yet now, somehow, once again I feel the pang of hunger.*"

"What's your choice of salad dressing?"

"*Well, it's not your run-of-the-mill marching band.*"

TOUR OF INSPECTION, 1926
(The King, accompanied by local officials)

"Hi, Billy. I'm the bluebird of happiness. I would have been here sooner, but I've had obligations."

"Good grief! What have you done to the body the good Lord gave you?"

"*We opened everything.*"

"Now, don't you fret, Winkler. There isn't one of us who hasn't spilled a few thousand gallons at one time or another."

"*Well! Let the good times roll!*"

"Say, I *like* that tune!"

"*Lot of new faces this summer.*"

AAHWK

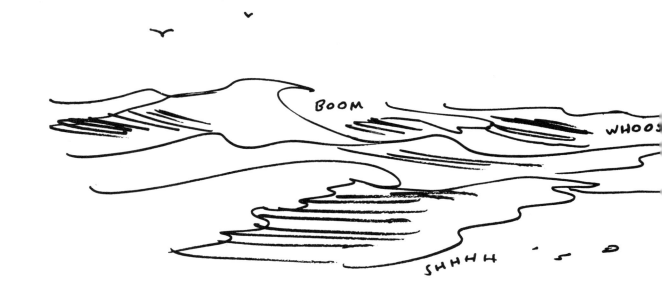

BOOM

WHOOS

SHHHH

"*Now, Edgar, you're not planning to play the fool tonight, are you?*"

"*Maybe you're too old to be pumping iron.*"

"*Why can't he just hibernate, like everybody else? Every year he has to give us his damn 'To sleep, perchance to dream.'*"

"For God's sake, don't join this firm."

"*I decided on brick, because my brothers had unfortunate experiences with other materials.*"

Aboard the Empress of Scotland

Venice

A flat tire at Lake Lucerne

Berlin

Alice and Don climbing Mont Blanc

Hotel Beaurivage (our room was on the other side)

The beach

Chamonix (not the top)

Nancy met a little Dutch girl in Amsterdam

A friend of Ed's from Amherst and his wife and her sister and aunt

Notre-Dame Cathedral, or Amiens

Passing the Caronia

"But I did get my act together. This is my act."

"*You know who I wrote in? You, Earl.*"

"*Pardon me, Madam. As I was going home just now, I couldn't help noticing you standing here, wet and weary and a little distraught, and it occurred to me that you, too, might be longing to get home, so . . .*"